Mental Models in Human-Computer Interaction

Research Issues About What the User of Software Knows

John M. Carroll and Judith Reitman Olson, *Editors*

Workshop on Software Human Factors: Users' Mental Models
Nancy Anderson, *Chair*
Committee on Human Factors
Commission on Behavioral and Social Sciences and Education
National Research Council

NATIONAL ACADEMY PRESS
Washington, D.C. 1987

NOTICE: The project that is the subject of this report was approved by the Governing Board of the National Research Council, whose members are drawn from the councils of the National Academy of Sciences, the National Academy of Engineering, and the Institute of Medicine. The members of the committee responsible for the report were chosen for their special competences and with regard for appropriate balance.

This report has been reviewed by a group other than the authors according to procedures approved by a Report Review Committee consisting of members of the National Academy of Sciences, the National Academy of Engineering, and the Institute of Medicine.

The National Academy of Sciences is a private, nonprofit, self-perpetuating society of distinguished scholars engaged in scientific and engineering research, dedicated to the furtherance of science and technology and to their use for the general welfare. Upon the authority of the charter granted to it by the Congress in 1863, the Academy has a mandate that requires it to advise the federal government on scientific and technical matters. Dr. Frank Press is president of the National Academy of Sciences.

The National Academy of Engineering was established in 1964, under the charter of the National Academy of Sciences, as a parallel organization of outstanding engineers. It is autonomous in its administration and in the selection of its members, sharing with the National Academy of Sciences the responsibility for advising the federal government. The National Academy of Engineering also sponsors engineering programs aimed at meeting national needs, encourages education and research, and recognizes the superior achievements of engineers. Dr. Robert M. White is president of the National Academy of Engineering.

The Institute of Medicine was established in 1970 by the National Academy of Sciences to secure the services of eminent members of appropriate professions in the examination of policy matters pertaining to the health of the public. The Institute acts under the responsibility given to the National Academy of Sciences by its congressional charter to be an adviser to the federal government and, upon its own initiative, to identify issues of medical care, research, and education. Dr. Samuel O. Thier is president of the Institute of Medicine.

The National Research Council was organized by the National Academy of Sciences in 1916 to associate the broad community of science and technology with the Academy's purposes of furthering knowledge and advising the federal government. Functioning in accordance with general policies determined by the Academy, the Council has become the principal operating agency of both the National Academy of Sciences and the National Academy of Engineering in providing services to the government, the public, and the scientific and engineering communities. The Council is administered jointly by both Academies and the Institute of Medicine. Dr. Frank Press and Dr. Robert M. White are chairman and vice chairman, respectively, of the National Research Council.

The United States government has at least a royalty-free, nonexclusive and irrevocable license throughout the world for government purposes to publish, translate, reproduce, deliver, perform, dispose of, and to authorize others so as to do, all or any portion of this work.
Available from
Committee on Human Factors
Commission on Behavioral and Social Sciences and Education
National Research Council
2101 Constitution Ave., N.W.
Washington, D.C. 20418
Printed in the United States of America

WORKSHOP ON SOFTWARE HUMAN FACTORS: USERS' MENTAL MODELS

NANCY ANDERSON (*Chair*), Department of Psychology, University of Maryland
ELIZABETH K. BAILEY, Consultant, Falls Church, Virginia
JOHN M. CARROLL, Watson Research Center, IBM Corporation, Yorktown Heights, New York
RICHARD J. JAGACINSKI, Department of Psychology, Ohio State University
DAVID R. LENOROVITZ, Computer Technology Associates, Inc., Englewood, Colorado
MARILYN MANTEI, Center for Machine Intelligence, Ann Arbor, Michigan
PHYLLIS REISNER, Almaden Research Center, IBM Research, San Jose, California
JUDITH REITMAN OLSON, Department of Computer and Information Systems, Graduate School of Business Administration, University of Michigan
JANET WALKER, Symbolics, Inc., Cambridge, Massachusetts
JOHN WHITESIDE, Digital Equipment Corporation, Nashua, New Hampshire
STANLEY DEUTSCH, Study Director

COMMITTEE ON HUMAN FACTORS 1986–1987

THOMAS B. SHERIDAN (*Chair*), Department of Mechanical Engineering, Massachusetts Institute of Technology
NANCY S. ANDERSON, Department of Psychology, University of Maryland
CLYDE H. COOMBS, Department of Psychology, University of Michigan
JEROME I. ELKIND, Information Systems, Xerox Corporation, Palo Alto
BARUCH B. FISCHHOFF, Decision Research (a branch of Perceptronics, Inc.), Eugene, Oregon
OSCAR GRUSKY, Department of Sociology, University of California, Los Angeles
ROBERT M. GUION, Department of Psychology, Bowling Green State University
DOUGLAS H. HARRIS, Anacapa Sciences, Santa Barbara, California
JULIAN HOCHBERG, Department of Psychology, Columbia University
THOMAS K. LANDAUER, Information Sciences Division, Bell Communication Research, Morristown, New Jersey
JUDITH REITMAN OLSON, Department of Computer and Information Systems, Graduate School of Business Administration, University of Michigan
RICHARD W. PEW (*Past Chair*), Computer and Information Sciences Division, Bolt Beranek and Newman Laboratories, Cambridge, Massachusetts
STOVER H. SNOOK, Liberty Mutual Research Center, Hopkinton, Massachusetts

ROBERT C. WILLIGES, Department of Industrial Engineering and Operations Research, Virginia Polytechnic Institute and State University
STANLEY DEUTSCH, Study Director (1984-1987)
HAROLD VAN COTT, Study Director

<u>ERRATUM</u> – p. vii

The Air Force Office of Scientific Research should have been included as one of the sponsors of the Committee on Human Factors.

Foreword

The Committee on Human Factors was established in October 1980 by the Commission on Behavioral and Social Sciences and Education of the National Research Council. The committee is sponsored by the Office of Naval Research, the Army Research Institute for the Behavioral and Social Sciences, the National Aeronautics and Space Administration, and the National Science Foundation. The principal objectives of the committee are to provide new perspectives on theoretical and methodological issues, to identify basic research needed to expand and strengthen the scientific basis of human factors, and to attract scientists both within and outside the field for interactive communication and to perform needed research. The goal of the committee is to provide a solid foundation of research as a base on which effective human factors practices can build.

Human factors issues arise in every domain in which humans interact with the products of a technological society. In order to perform its role effectively, the committee draws on experts from a wide range of scientific and engineering disciplines. Members of the committee include specialists in such fields as psychology, engineering, biomechanics, physiology, medicine, cognitive sciences, machine intelligence, computer sciences, sociology, education, and human factors engineering. Other disciplines are represented in the working groups, workshops, and symposia. Each of these disciplines contributes to the basic data, theory and methods required to improve the scientific basis of human factors.

FOREWORD

Contents

Preface	xi
Abstract	xv
Introduction	3
Models of What, Held by Whom?	3
Types of Representations of Users' Knowledge	5
Simple Sequences	6
Methods and Ways to Choose Among Them	8
Mental Models	12
Surrogates	13
Metaphor Models	13
Glass Box Models	14
Network Representations of the System	15
Comparisons	17
How Users' Knowledge Affects Their Performance	19
Chaos and Misconception in Both Novices and Experts	20
Skilled Performance	21
Applying What We Know of the User's Knowledge to Practical Problems	23
Designing Interfaces	24
User Training	26
Research Recommendations	29
References	34

FOREWORD x

Preface

There has been a long-standing problem with inferring the causes of complex behavior. Mental events are not directly observable; they must be inferred from overt behavior. Behaviorists reject mental events as legitimate scientific concepts. More recently, however, developments in cognitive science and artificial intelligence, in which mental events are specifically modeled and found to have measurable correlates in behavior, have brought the concepts back into fashion. These mental events, their description and postulated interrelationships, are the subject of this report. We focus specifically on the mental events that are postulated to occur as someone learns or performs complex tasks on computer software.

From the point of view of cognitive science, users of computer software systems base their behavior on stored knowledge about particular sequences of actions, on general rules about how to accomplish certain tasks, or on a mental model (an underlying understanding of how the system works). Knowing what the user knows about or expects from a system has implications for both design and training purposes. From a design point of view, the system could be designed to fit the user's goals in accomplishing tasks or could display enough of how it works to make accomplishing a task easy to understand. From the training point of view, users could be given instructions and exercises that clearly present sequences, rules, and/or a model in order to make learning and performing easy.

At present, there is no satisfactory way of describing what the user knows. There is no way to characterize the differences among users of various systems as they go through the process of developing an awareness and understanding of how the system works or how a given task is to be performed. Consequently, the Committee on Human Factors conducted a two-day workshop on May 15 and 16, 1984, to determine means for achieving a better understanding of what users know and its implications for system and software design as well as user training. This workshop was a continuation of the committee's efforts to define research needs in the area of software human factors. Ten nationally known researchers on software design, cognitive psychology, and human factors met to discuss the issues having to do with what a user of software knows.

As background for this workshop, John M. Carroll wrote an invited paper entitled "Mental Models and Software Human Factors: An Overview." This was distributed to all participants in advance of the meeting. In turn, the workshop members prepared short two- to three-page position papers addressing additional topics and issues that they believed were important and warranted discussion at the workshop. Much of the discussion at the workshop centered on sifting through the many definitions of the term *mental model*, gathering ideas from among the variety of methods used to represent users' knowledge about software systems.

This report was prepared by merging the ideas generated by the workshop members with those in Carroll's paper. It includes his central organization and literature review, adds more recent information, and clarifies the distinction between mental models and task representations. This report was then distributed to workshop participants for changes and additions.

This report is written for the researcher concerned with the psychology of performance of complex tasks and for the practitioner who would like to use information about how the user thinks about both the task and the system in the design of computer software, its documentation, or training for its use. Most of the research on these questions has used software-based text-editing tasks as a domain and looked at the mental models people are purported to build of only simple devices. The results should be generalized to even more complex tasks, such as process control, tactical decision making, project planning, and graphics design; but their scope has not been tested. The exclusion of these kinds of tasks is not to be taken as an indication that the research reported cannot cover these more complex tasks. But their scope is an important research need.

    Judith Reitman Olson

Abstract

Users of software systems acquire knowledge about the system and how to use it through experience, training, and imitation. Currently, there is a great deal of debate about exactly what users know about software. This knowledge may include one or more of the following:

- simple rules that prescribe a sequence of actions that apply under certain conditions;
- general methods that fit certain general situations and goals; and
- *mental models,* knowledge of the components of a system, their interconnection, and the processes that change the components; knowledge that forms the basis for users being able to construct reasonable actions; and explanations about why a set of actions is appropriate.

Discovering what users know and how these different forms of knowledge fit together in learning and performance is important. It applies to the problem of designing systems and training programs so that the systems are easy to use and the learning is efficient. Research on the effects of different representations on ultimate performance is mixed. Research on exactly what users know is scattered. Analytical methods and techniques for representing what the user knows are sparse but growing.

This report reviews current work and through the review, identifies several important research needs:

- Detail what kinds of mental representations people have of systems that allow them to behave appropriately in using the software.
- Detail what a mental model would consist of and how a person would use it to decide what action to take next.
- Produce evidence that people have and use mental models.
- Determine the behaviors that would demonstrate a mental model's form and the operations used on the model.
- Explore alternative views of goal-directed representations (e.g., so-called sequence/method representations) and detail the behavior predicted from them.
- Expand the types of mental representations that may exist to include those that may not be mechanistic, such as algebraic and visual systems.
- Determine how people intermix different representations in producing behavior.
- Explore how knowledge about systems is acquired.
- Determine how individual differences have an impact on learning of and performance on systems.
- Explore the design of training sequences for systems.
- Provide systems designers with tools to help them develop systems that evoke "good" representations in users.
- Expand the task domain of this research to include more complex software.

Mental Models in Human-Computer Interaction: Research Issues About What the User of Software Knows

INTRODUCTION

Discovering what the users of a computer software system do know and should know are important goals in current research on human-computer interaction. Research on the kinds of knowledge people have when they use computers, including the concept of a mental model of the system, is one of the major topics that is bringing the field of human-computer interaction from the tradition of human factors closer to that of experimental/cognitive psychology. Traditional human factors work has focused principal attention on behavior and performance itself, and has avoided the problem of describing the conceptual causes and effects of that behavior. On the other hand, while academic cognitive psychology does concern itself with theoretical interpretations of mental processes, it has focused on narrowly restricted mental processes, such as particular aspects of learning, memory, problem solving, or planning, and has studied them in the context of highly controlled and contrived laboratory tasks. The study of knowledge representations of users of computer-based systems affords an opportunity to explore both the theoretical base of behavior as well as specific behaviors in tasks that involve many different cognitive processes in concert.

Because a number of researchers are concerned with mental representations, and because this topic has an impact on cognitive psychology and software human factors, there is an emerging need to clarify the concepts underlying *knowledge representation* and *mental models* as they apply to human-computer interaction. We intend to fill this need by reviewing relevant current research and presenting a preliminary framework of the kinds of mental representations of procedures people might have.

MODELS OF WHAT, HELD BY WHOM?

Several key distinctions need to be recognized in discussing mental representations and mental models in human-computer interaction. For example, various individuals are concerned with using or designing a piece of software, and they hold different conceptions of it. These individuals include the user, the software engineer, the human factors analyst, and the cognitive psychologist. Furthermore, there are different aspects of the system to be known: the *task*, knowing what the goal is and in general what subtasks need to be accomplished to achieve the goal; the *system interface*, knowing how to accomplish the sequence of subtasks in this system, given the data presentation and interaction languages of this system; and the *system architecture*, knowing the way the data are stored, the internal processes the interactions invoke, and in general how the system works.

Confusion has surrounded the term *mental model* because different authors have referred to different owners of the models (the user, the software engineer, etc.) and are not clear as to what the model actually represents (the task, the architecture, etc.).

For example, some researchers and human factors analysts acknowledge that it is important to know the way users themselves are built and work, what their memory limits are, their common strategies in problem solving, their individual differences, and so on, in order to build useful, usable software. A system that requires the user to remember a list of 100 codes that represent areas of the country or the types of transactions that are required (as in some airline or automobile reservation systems) is predictably difficult because our model of the user includes a long-term memory that is confused by similar meaningless items. These researchers have sometimes used the term *mental model* to refer to the model that they, as researchers, have of the user's mental architecture.

Similarly, software engineers have ideas about what the user wants to do and how the system itself is structured that dictate how they will program the system and how it will operate to serve the users' needs. Engineers have mental models of their design.

This highlights another distinction, that between *descriptive* and *prescriptive* representations. Researchers want to be able to analyze what the user currently knows so they can explain why he or she is having difficulty, which aspects are learned and which are confused, and so on. In this case, they are using a descriptive model, one that tells us what the user knows. Designers, however, want to construct a model of what the user should know. This representation could be used to analyze, for example, whether a proposed system will be too difficult to learn or where the errors might be. And, in designing commands and screen presentations, designers would like to invoke a model in the user that fits the dialog; they would like to get the user to build a mental model of the system that fits what the users have to do to operate the system. Descriptive models are those held by the researcher to approximate what the user does know; prescriptive models are those held by the designer to approximate what the user should know.

The concern of this report, however, is the representation that the user has of how a computer system works. Furthermore, since a mental model may be only one way of describing the knowledge that a user has about a system, this report is broadened to include all of what a user knows about using a particular piece of software, including how to use it and how it works.

What users know differs in several important dimensions. It differs according to the sophistication of the user. For example, a user who is a programmer might have a very different understanding of a piece of software than a person with no programming experience. Also, multiple mental models or several representations at different levels of abstraction might coexist within the same individual. For example, a person who both designed and later used a system might develop two somewhat compartmentalized understandings of the system. Analogous distinctions arise if we consider different task environments. For example, the representation elicited for routine skilled behavior might differ substantively from that elicited when a person tries to recover from an error or otherwise solve problems (e.g., Rasmussen, 1983).

Because understanding what the user knows has practical importance for designing software and its training, and because it has theoretical importance in understanding people as they generally perform complex cognitive tasks, this report considers only the representations the users have when using software—representations of the task being performed, the user-system interface, and the system architecture.

TYPES OF REPRESENTATIONS OF USERS' KNOWLEDGE

There are three basic types of representations that have been formulated to characterize what a user of software knows. The most elementary is a *simple sequence* of overt actions that fit a particular situation. The second is a more complex and general characterization, the knowledge of *methods*. This kind of representation of the user's behavior incorporates general goals, the subgoals associated with it, a set of methods that could be brought to bear to accomplish the subgoals, and, finally, sequences of operators for those methods. Both of these conceptualizations are task-oriented in that they contain no theory of how the software or system works or what the user's actions do internally to produce the results.

The third, the *mental model*,[1] is knowledge of how the system works, what its components are, how they are related, what the internal processes are, and how they affect the components. It is this conceptualization that allows the user not only to construct actions for novel tasks but also to explain why a particular action produces the results it does.

SIMPLE SEQUENCES

Users often have no knowledge of the underlying system or even general rules for getting things done. Novices, in particular, resort to a learning method that borders on rote memorization. They learn sequences of actions that will get the system to do common types of tasks. For example, in using the operating system on the Michigan Terminal System to print the contents of a text file with the laser printer, many users merely memorize the nearly nonsense strings:

$RUN *textform scards = pc:fw.macros + *file* spunch = -x *'run a program called "textform" with input from a master file of parameters plus the input file, send the output to a temporary file called "x"'*

$RUN *pagepr scards = -x par = onesided *'run a program called "pagepr" with input from the temporary file "x" so that the output is printed on only one side of each page'*

where the only free parameter to be entered is the name of the *file* after the "+" in the first "scards" designation. Similarly, some word processors require the user to memorize short, common

---

[1]This is a subset of the knowledge Rouse and Morris (1986) call mental models. We would include knowledge that helps the user to explain the function and states of the system and to predict its future behavior. We would not include descriptions of its purpose and form, information that seems shallow and unhelpful in a performance context.

command sequences to accomplish certain repetitive actions, such as "<cntl> XME" to exit, and "<cntl> XLA" to enact the printing sequence. A good clue as to how often users rely on these simple sequences is to note the cheat sheets that they keep available when they are using software, or the notes made and often stuck to the side of the cathode-ray tube to remind the user of some commands that are commonly used but difficult to remember.

Young (1983) described one way in which users think about a calculator, as simple sequences or sets of task-action pairs. A *task* includes something the user wishes to accomplish (e.g., an arithmetic calculation or formula evaluation), which is associated with an *action,* or what the user must do in order to accomplish the task (e.g., key presses on a calculator). This knowledge is in the form of paired associates, and like the sequences to print a file described above, it has simple slots that indicate the free parameters the user must designate to fit the current situation.

A second description of simple sequences of actions is the keystroke model (Card et al., 1980a,b, 1983; Embley et al., 1978). The analyses in the keystroke models contain notations that describe what sequences of actions users make in invoking simple commands: the keystrokes, mouse movements and so on. In Card et al. (1980a,b, 1983) keystroke analysis, the analyst assumes that the user needs time to make each act in producing the command: a time to make a keystroke, a time to point with a mouse, a time to move the hands from the keyboard to the mouse or back, and a time to mentally prepare each command and its parameters. The analysis assumes that users must retrieve each command sequence from their memory, incurring a pause for mental preparation, and then execute the components of the command, pausing for additional mental preparation times before each command word, each parameter, and each delimiter (such as pressing a parenthesis, return, or other type of operator). For example, a command sequence for using a line-oriented editor to search a file for an error and fix it:

s /f "errorstring"

'search the whole file for an error'

a 16 "oldstring" newstring"

'alter line 16 so that the old string is replaced with the new string'

would include mental preparations before each line and before each parameter, such as "/f" and "16," and the strings to be searched for and replaced. Analysis proceeds by attaching a constant time for each keystroke, movement, or mental preparation, affording a prediction of how long the formulation and execution of each command would normally require.

In the same spirit, Reisner (1984) assumes that the user needs a fixed amount of time to make each individual act in producing a command. Instead of one mental preparation time, however, Reisner (1984) posits specific mental acts (e.g., retrieving from long-term memory, calculating a number, copying a number), each of which takes a different length of time. The analyst assumes (or knows from prior experimentation) how the various parameters are related (e.g., the time to calculate a number will be greater than the time to copy that number from a display) without specifying each time exactly. Simple algebra is then used to predict which of various whole design alternatives, or which of various user methods, will require the shortest time to perform.

These analyses of simple sequences serve to facilitate both comparison of existing software packages for the one that will require the shortest time to perform and the design and development of new system languages.

METHODS AND WAYS TO CHOOSE AMONG THEM

Users not only elicit simple sequences to fit simple situations by rote; they sometimes also choose among various possible general methods that fit a particular situation.[2]

A number of investigators have studied the organization of more general actions as a function of task goals in the domain of programming. A general finding is that skilled programmers recognize aspects of particular situations and select general actions appropriate to them. For example, individual statements or sets of lines of code in a program are "chunked" into higher-order task-relevant structures. Skilled programmers can recall at a glance more lines of code than novice programmers (Adelson, 1981; McKeithen et al., 1981; Shneiderman, 1980). This is consistent

---

[2]These methods are similar to the procedures remembered and used in the stage of "deciding and testing actions" in supervisory control tasks, described by Sheridan et al. (1986).

with prior studies of expertise and the organization of memory (Chase and Simon, 1973; Egan and Schwartz, 1979; Reitman, 1976). These studies suggest that in the skilled programmer's knowledge base there is a mapping between chunks of actions or methods (that often go together) and general task features, so that the actions will be recalled and used at appropriate times in the future. These chunks reflect a developed, deeper understanding of routine programs, which are useful to a programmer writing programs. Similarly, Ehrlich and Soloway (1984) have shown that skilled programmers tend to employ patterns of actions, called plans, consisting of routinely occurring sequences of programming statements.

Furthermore, by examining the structure of recall protocols, McKeithen et al. (1981) determined that skilled programmers organize their vocabulary of programming statements more stereotypically than do novice programmers. It appears that with expertise, the users' understanding converges to a similar set of representations of concepts in the programming language. Data base designers reveal mental organizations that become increasingly homogeneous with greater expertise (Smelcer, 1986).

A more complete theory about what the user knows about how to accomplish a particular task is the GOMS model (Card et al., 1983). GOMS is an acronym that stands for the elements of what the user knows: the goals, the operators, the methods, and selection rules. In the GOMS model, the user has a certain goal to accomplish (such as editing a manuscript that has been marked up). The user recognizes that this large goal can be broken into a set of subgoals (such as finding each editing mark and making the requisite changes). Subgoals are broken down into smaller and smaller subgoals until they match a basic set of methods, that is, sequences of operations that satisfy a small subgoal.

The GOMS model states that users have some rules by which they choose the method that will fit the current situation. For example, users may know that there are several methods that can be used to find the first place in the manuscript to be edited: using the search function with a distinguishing string to be found, using the page-forward key until the target page is found visually, or using the cursor key to find the specific target location visually. People will choose whether to use the search, page-forward, or cursor key method depending on how far away the next editing target is assumed to be. Each of these methods is made up of certain operators, key presses, and hand motions, as specified in the keystroke model described above in the discussion of simple sequences.

A number of empirical studies have shown that the predictions of GOMS and the keystroke model are reasonably accurate, and that sometimes one can even use the same time parameters across applications. Card et al. (1983) showed that their parameters for keystrokes and mental processing time were similar across text processors, operating systems, and graphics packages. Olson and Nilsen (1987) extended the analysis to show that the basic parameters applied well to spreadsheet software. However, additional time parameters were required. One was to account for the time it took users to scan the screen (for example, to find on the screen the coordinates of a particular value in a spreadsheet). A second time parameter was required to account for the time it takes the user to choose between methods: the more methods to choose from, the longer the pause before executing a simple sequence in a command.

Command grammars use a different analytic representation, but are analyzing the same kinds of mental events. The command language grammar (CLG) (Moran, 1981) and Backus normal form (BNF) (Reisner, 1981, 1984) have been used to describe the organization of sequences of actions that fulfill goals. These grammars are sets of rules that show the different ways in which an "alphabet" of actions can be formed to produce acceptable "sentences" that are understandable to a system or a device.

For example, Reisner (1981, 1984) treats user actions that are acceptable to the system as a language. She describes the structure of this language as a BNF grammar. Figure 1 shows a sample of what in this formalism are called *rewrite rules*. At the higher levels are the user's task goals and the possible methods that can achieve the goal. This is presumably a representation of the components of plans the user has ready to evoke to fill an overall task goal. Below these are the varieties of action sequences that can be elicited in a method. The top several lines of Figure 1 are similar to the goals/subgoals and methods of the GOMS analysis; the lower levels are similar to the keystroke model sequences.

Compared to GOMS, this representation more compactly shows the alternative ways to accomplish a task or to enact a series of keystrokes; GOMS requires a new method for each alternative. While various methods (represented as sentences from such a grammar) can be compared to see which takes less time, a grammatical representation is less adequate than GOMS in that it lacks any way to represent how a user selects the method appropriate for the current situation.

Use Dn	..>Identify first line + enter Dn command + press ENTER
Identify first line	..>Get first line on screen + Move cursor to first line
Get first line on screen	..>Use "locate" strategy use scroll strategy
"Locate" strategy	..>Move cursor to command Input field + type "locate" command + press ENTER
Move cursor to command Input field	..>Use cursor keys press PFCURSOR null
Type locate command	..>Type "locate" keyword + type line number
Type locate keyword	..>L+O+C L L+O+C+A+T+E
Type line number	..>Type number

FIGURE 1 A command grammar representation of actions necessary to edit a line using a word processor. Rewrite rules applied to this domain are compact definitions of the many acceptable ways to get something done in a particular command language. One reads these rules from left to right; the left-hand terms are made up of the elements listed on the right-hand side. Elements connected by a "+" are executed in sequence, elements connected by a "—" represent alternative ways of invoking the same goal. For example, "Use Dn" consists of identifying the first line, *then* entering the "Dn" command, and *then* pressing enter. Typing the locate keyword, however, includes typing "LOC," "L," or "LOCATE." Source: Reisner (1984:53).

The language format of grammars, however, allows the use of standard sentence complexity measures to predict some aspects of user behavior: the more rules, the long it takes a user to learn; the greater the sentence (sequence) complexity, the longer the pauses between keystrokes; the more terminal symbols in the language, the harder the language is to learn. These predictions have not been fully tested, and there is some suggestion in the literature about language understanding that these measures do not adequately predict how difficult it is to understand sentences (Fodor et al., 1974; Miller, 1962). The formalism, however, allows a number of intriguing predictive possibilities for understanding and recalling command languages. See Reisner (1983) for a discussion of the potential value of such grammars.

MENTAL MODELS

In its most generic application, the term *mental model* could be applied to any set of mental events, but few if anyone would claim such meaning for the word *model*. Somewhat narrower in meaning, the term could be used for any thought process in which there are defined inputs and outputs to a believable process which operates on the inputs to produce outputs. In this sense, one could have a mental model of one's own behavior ("If I do this, then that will happen"), another person's behavior, the input-output characteristics of any software process run on a computer, or any information process mediated by people or machines. It could be a series of paired associates by which the user predicts, through a causal chain, outputs of a process given its inputs.

Given these general possibilities for the term mental model, it is most commonly used to refer to a representation (in the head) of a physical system or software being run on a computer, with some plausible cascade of causal associations connecting the input to the output. Accordingly, the user's mental model of a system is here defined as a rich and elaborate structure, reflecting the user's understanding of what the system contains, how it works, and why it works that way. It can be conceived as knowledge about the system sufficient to permit the user to mentally try out actions before choosing one to execute. A key feature of a mental model is that it can be "run" with trial, exploratory inputs and observed for its resultant behavior (Sheridan et al., 1986).

Mental models are used during learning (such as using an analogy to begin to understand how the system works), in problem solving (such as in trying to extricate oneself from an error or performing a novel task), and when the user is reflecting on or attempting to rationalize or explain the system's behavior.

Users are typically described as using a mechanistic model; that is, the user is assumed to have a conceptual "machine" whose simulated function matches the actual target machine in some way.[3] Three general kinds of models are called surrogates (Young, 1983), metaphors (Carroll and Thomas, 1982), and glass boxes (DuBoulay et al., 1981). A fourth kind of model, the network model, is a composite, blending the features of surrogates and glass boxes.

---

[3]This may be more due to the fact that researchers are good at describing mechanistic models than to the fact that it is the only kind of model people have. In fact, exploration of other representations is an important research need.

Surrogates

A surrogate is a conceptual analysis that perfectly mimics the target system's input/output behavior and that does not assume that the way in which output is produced in the surrogate is the same process as that in the target system. It is a system that behaves the same, but is not assumed to be isomorphic in its internal workings. Thus, while the surrogate always provides the right answer (the one that the target system would have generated), it offers no means of illuminating the real underlying causal basis for the answer. It is a good, complete analogy that may allow the user to construct appropriate behavior in a novel situation, but it does not help the user explain whey the system behaves the way it does.

Young (1983) noted that it is very difficult to construct an adequate surrogate, even for a fairly simple system like a handheld calculator. This raises the question of whether people ever hold surrogates in their minds, even for simple devices.

Metaphor Models

A metaphor model is a direct comparison between the target system and some other system already known to the user. A common example, referred to widely in the literature, is the metaphor that "a text editor is a typewriter." Many investigators have observed that new users spontaneously refer to this typewriter metaphor during early learning about text processors (Bott, 1979; Carroll and Thomas, 1982; Douglas and Moran, 1983; Mack et al., 1983). The explanations people offer for system behavior are often couched in the vocabulary of the metaphor. Furthermore, the extent to which knowledge in the metaphor source domain matches the target domain correlates with performance. That is, the task-action pairs that fit both the metaphor source and the target system are easy to learn; those that do not are often learned last or remain constant sources of error. For example, learners have less trouble learning how to use character keys than the backspace and carriage return keys; the latter typically operate differently in text processors than they do in typewriters.

Unlike surrogates, metaphor models are easy to construct or learn, and they provide explanations of why the system behaves as it does. However, metaphors vary greatly in accuracy. For example, "the interface is a desktop" seems less accurate than "values are put into storage locations."

One difficulty with using metaphors in analyzing users' behavior with computers is it is difficult to find out what the users' metaphors are. As Young (1983) put it, a metaphor analysis exchanges the problem of describing what the user knows about the target system for the problem of describing what the user knows about the metaphor source. For example, user have to know enough about pipelines for the metaphor "a flow chart is a pipeline" to be useful. In addition, metaphors that map one domain perfectly into another are rare. Consequently, metaphors can sometimes be misleading as well as helpful. The hydrodynamic metaphor for electric current, for example, is only good for a limited subset of phenomena, and is misleading for many others. Similarly, the typewriter metaphor for a word processor helps with some actions (like using the backspace key), but interferes with the learning of others (like the return key) (Douglas and Moran, 1983).

Glass Box Models

Glass box models lie between metaphors and surrogates. They are surrogates in that they are perfect mimics of the target system. But they are metaphors in that they offer some semantic interpretation for the internal components. For example, Mayer (1976) discusses a glass box mimic for a BASIC-like programming language. This glass box is not simply a surrogate, because its components are presented via metaphors (input as a ticket window, storage as a file cabinet). It can be run to perfectly predict outputs from inputs, but it can also be interpreted via these metaphors. Yet it is also not a simple metaphor; it is a composite metaphor (Carroll and Thomas, 1982; Rumelhart and Norman, 1981). It does not merely exchange the target system for a metaphor source in toto; it uses aspects of several metaphors to provide the surrogate behavior.

Glass boxes have been used primarily in a prescriptive context rather than in a descriptive one. Mayer's (1976) glass box is not a mental structure that was discovered; it is a mental structure that was taught to the user (e.g., subjects were instructed to think of input as a ticket window). Studies of prescriptive conceptual models tell us something about what kinds of models are useful, and about models that people could generate. On the other hand, they can validate prescriptive models that help users of complex systems when it is hard for the user to deduce an adequate representation merely from experience.

Network Representations of the System

Network representations contain the *states* a system can be in and the *actions* the user can take that change the system to another state (Miller, 1985). One particular type of network representation, the generalized transition network (GTN), contains detailed descriptions of what the system does (Kieras and Polson, 1983). GTN's are state transition diagrams that represent the visible states of the system (i.e., the display on the screen) as nodes, and the actions the user can take at each state (the commands or menu choices) as arcs. The connected nodes and arcs form a network that shows the sequence of states that follow user actions at each point in the software interaction. GTN's and other network diagrams are often used as tools in system development, to give the designer a picture to refer to in order to keep track of what can be done at every state in the transaction. Figure 2 illustrates a portion of one of these networks for the actions that can be taken when a user enters a system and loads the word processing application.

Networks can also be used to describe what the user knows about the system (Olson, 1987). Olson (1987) suggests that GTNs be used to represent users' knowledge of system states and allowable actions; these can be compared to the GTN of the actual target system to measure the user's level of learning or understanding. Examination of the parts of the real GTN that are missing in the user's representation could indicated areas in which learning or remembering certain functions is difficult.

The GTN is like a surrogate representation in that it does not give an underlying explanation about why the elements are related in the way that they are nor how the internal system components behave. Nor is there any indication of the purpose these actions fill toward a user's goal. It does, however, represent what the user knows about how the system works in simple stimulus-reponse terms. A GTN displays the simple response that can be expected from the system given each action the user takes. And, importantly to the user, knowledge of these actions and their consequences can be useful when the user must solve problems, either when an error has just occurred or when a novel goal has arisen and the user needs to decide on an appropriate sequence of actions.

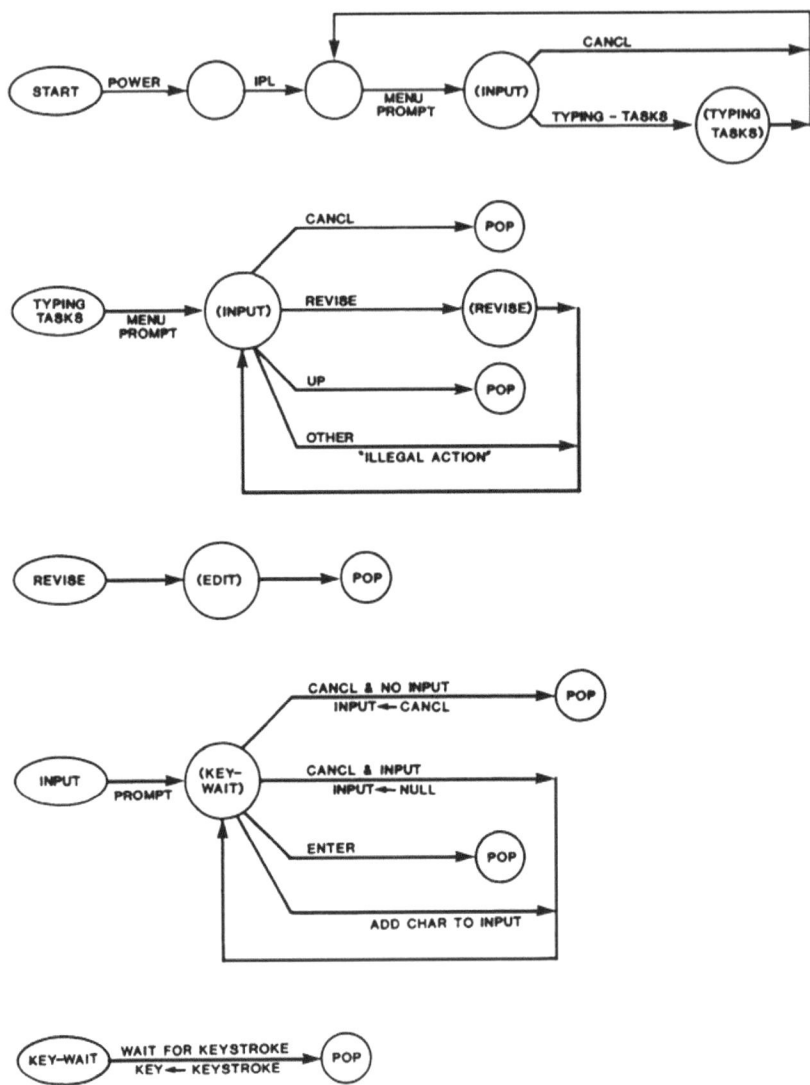

FIGURE 2 A generalized transition network (GTN) representation of part of the task of editing a document. Circles represent states or tasks, arcs represent the connections between states, and labels to the arcs represent the actions the user takes. Source: Kieras and Polson (1983:104).

COMPARISONS

It is useful to consider the relation between sequence/method representations and mental models. People undoubtedly have both kinds of knowledge when they use computing systems. But research on these two approaches is largely complementary in that the kinds of questions addressed about one kind of representation have been different from those about the other. Briefly, the sequence/method representations are more analytic in that they can predict behavior (except errors) in some detail. Although the sequence/method approach has not typically dealt with predicting user errors, attempts have been made to show how user learning takes place. The mental models approach, on the other hand, accounts for errors as well as accurate behavior in novel and standard situations, but does not predict the details of behavior well nor how the models are learned.

Sequence/method representations, because they are composed of goal-action pairs, by their very nature predict how knowledge is used. To date they have represented only how to accomplish routine tasks (in which all the goal-subgoal and subgoal-action relations have been worked out) but have little or nothing to say about how knowledge is used in nonroutine tasks, such as in recovering from an error or behaving in an entirely unfamiliar situation. They do not have much generality in their conditions. And, there is no posited mechanism for problem solving when a new situation fits several general condition-action pairs. Without this mechanism, these analyses cannot account for errors. Some attempt has been made to account for how sequence/method representations are learned. Lewis (1986) provides an account of how users might acquire goal-action knowledge after they watch another person use the system. Through several simple heuristics that link actions to probable causes, the user begins to build a reasonable set of rules. The acquisition of rules is detailed by

Lewis (1986), but the further learning in fine-tuning those rules is not covered. Kieras and Bovair (1986) do not explain original learning per se, but have shown that learning a new system is speeded up if the user is familiar with another system that has many of the same rules in common. Neither of these approaches addresses the continued learning that goes on as the user acquires or discovers new strategies for efficiency.

Research on mental models, on the other hand, has not concentrated on the details of how a user uses a mental model nor how it is acquired. Douglas and Moran (1983) have produced the most detailed analysis of the behavior of a user who has a mental model. They examined the analogy of "a text processor is a typewriter" by noting the typewriter condition-action sequences that matched and mismatched those in the new system. Those condition-action pairs that matched were learned easily and quickly, and those that did not match produced continued errors and pauses. Other researchers have attempted to make the analysis of the behavior of the user who has a mental model more specific and revealing (Foley and Williges, 1982; Moran, 1983; Payne and Green, 1983). What is missing from these analyses, however, is how users use their mental models to come up with a set of appropriate actions. There are likely to be some very interesting cognitive actions going on in the pause between the presentation of the problem (e.g., the feedback from the screen after an error) and the choice of the next action.

Most of the empirical work on the effectiveness of mental models and the predictive power of sequence/method analyses has been at a gross behavioral level. The studies of experts' chunking of information (Chase and Simon, 1973, for example) are almost completely empirical; they focus entirely on the acquisition of the condition part of a condition-action pair and offer little basis for theory. The grammatical approaches often hold a key assumption: that the fewer actions there are per task, the cognitively simpler the task. Recent work has raised questions about the accuracy of this assumption (Olson and Nilsen, 1988; Rosson, 1983). There are occasions when a task has a few actions, but the planning and calculating necessary to make those actions is difficult.

Moran has described a number of connections and contrasts between sequence/method and mental model approaches. The GOMS analysis (a methods analysis) and CLG (a blend of method and mental model) sprang from common theoretical roots. Indeed,

GOMS can be viewed as a simplified and more parameterized, compiled CLG. Moran (1981), however, stresses two contrasts. First, where CLG incorporates a limited mental model of the system in its semantic level, GOMS incorporates no mental model whatsoever. GOMS incorporates only the knowledge required to perform a task. Second, where the focus of CLG is the functional description of various levels of user knowledge and the mappings between these levels, the focus of GOMS is the sequencing of operators and the time requirements for each. The bottom line for GOMS is predicting performance times.

Kieras and Polson (1983) simulate users' behavior on particular computer systems. They have two representations in their simulations, which with an additional twist can be viewed in much the same spirit as Moran's (1981) view of the relation between CLG and GOMS. In the Kieras and Polson (1983) model, a job-task representation describes the person's understanding of when and how to carry out tasks (very much like GOMS). The simulated user's behavior is responded to by a simulation of the system, a device representation, which is a GTN of the states and transitions between them in the system. Some knowledge of this system behavior, a mental GTN, can represent what the user knows about the system—a thin, surrogate mental model. The former GOMS-like representation is the user's knowledge that produces performance, while the latter, the mental GTN, could be the user's theory during learning, problem solving, and explaining how the system works.

HOW USERS' KNOWLEDGE AFFECTS THEIR PERFORMANCE

The discussion up to this point has treated what the user knows as a static structure. While we have alluded to its underlying role in behavior (learning, problem solving, explanation, skill), we have not focused on these behavioral processes per se. Nevertheless, this aspect is critical both to assessing the empirical content of current analyses and to determining how these analyses might be applied to practical problems like the design of user interfaces and training materials.

CHAOS AND MISCONCEPTION IN BOTH NOVICES AND EXPERTS

Learning involves internalizing, constructing, or otherwise attaining a representation of the system being learned. How does this process proceed and what are its early results? The summary picture is of a halting and often somewhat nonconvergent process of problem solving and invention (e.g., Bott, 1979; Mack et al., 1983; Rumelhart and Norman, 1981). Indeed, the models that learners spontaneously form are incomplete, inconsistent, unstable in time, overly simple, and often rife with superstition.

A person may develop an understanding that is adequate for simple cases but that does not extend to more complex cases. For example, Mayer and Bayman (1981) found that users of calculators often believed that evaluation only occurs when the equals key is pressed. Scandura et al. (1976) describe a student who concluded that the equals key and plus keys on a calculator had no function because they caused no visible change in the display. Norman (1983) describes learners who superstitiously pressed the clear key on calculators several times, when a single key press would do. People learning to use a simple programmable robot developed wrong analogical models of its behavior that they accepted without testing until the models failed to predict the actions the robot took (Shrager and Klahr, 1983). Mantei (1982) found that users performing a task in a menu-based retrieval system developed and maintained simplistic sequences of actions that were eventually ineffective in accomplishing their search goals.

Chaotic and misconceived conceptual models are not merely an issue of early learning and something that users outgrow. Experienced users hold them as well. For example, Mayer and Bayman (1981) asked students to predict the outcomes of key press sequences on a calculator. Even though all of the students were experienced in the use of calculators, their predictions varied considerably. For example, some predicted that an evaluation occurs immediately after a number key is pressed, some predicted that evaluation occurs immediately after an operation (e.g., plus) key is pressed, and some predicted that an evaluation occurs immediately after equals is pressed.

Rosson (1983) found that even experienced users of a text editing system often had rather limited command repertoires, routinely employing nonoptimal methods (such as making repeated local changes instead of a single global change). Even in large powerful systems, most of the activity involves the use of only a very small portion of the system. In the case of UNIX, for example, 20 of the available 400 commands accounted for about 70 percent of the usage (Kraut et al., 1983). Like the Mayer and Bayman work (1981), this suggests that even an extensive amount of experience does not necessarily lead the user to a complete, consistent, or even correct conceptual model. There are some things about a system that most users never learn.

SKILLED PERFORMANCE

Human performance analyses have been well developed in vehicular control (e.g., aircraft, ship, automobile) and target pursuit tasks. Many of these analyses explicitly hypothesize a mental model of the system being operated (e.g., Baron and Levison, 1980; Jagacinski and Miller, 1978; Pew and Baron, 1983; Veldhuyzen and Stassen, 1976). In these cases, the mental model is used to anticipate the response of a dynamic system and hence to overcome the deleterious effects of time delays either from other humans or hardware. These models have produced good descriptions and predictions of human performance.

Because these models deal with spatio-temporal trajectories, their applicability is limited to continuous detection and movement tasks. In contrast, episodic models of movement that incorporate an additional, abstract level of description in terms of discrete situation-action pairs have much in common with goal-action models in human-computer interaction. Discrete representational and data reduction techniques developed for episodic skilled performance (Jagacinski et al., in press; Miller, 1985) may prove useful in the domain of human-computer interaction. Software user tasks do, however, typically involve a larger set of situation-action pairs than is covered in human performance analyses, and they probably involve more varied categorization and planning by the human operator. Whether they can be generalized to the greater cognitive complexity of human-computer interaction tasks is an open question.

If we assume that knowledge of simple sequences is in the form of goal-action pairs, then we should be able to apply what we know from traditional verbal learning studies about the retention of paired associates (e.g., Hilgard and Bower, 1975; Postman and

Stark, 1969) to predict which systems will be easy to learn and what kinds of errors will occur. For example, presumably, those systems that have few paired associates to be learned or those that have distinct, nonconfusable goal-action pairs will be easy to learn and remember.

Landauer et al. (1983), Barnard et al. (1981), and others have explored certain aspects of this issue with mixed results. Landauer et al. (1984) discuss the difficulties of constructing command names that are natural, that is, those that would have existing goal-action paired associates in memory and ready to transfer easily to a new task. They argue that if one incorporates command names generated by naive users, these names are natural but often are not distinctive enough to allow users to keep from getting them confused among each other. Preexisting paired associates can help transfer, but if they are not distinct paired associates as a set (e.g., A-B may be good until it must be learned along with A-C), the confusion can offset any positive effect from their naturalness.

Polson and Kieras (1984, 1985) embody the GOMS model in a production system-based simulation of users' behavior while using software. This is a very concrete representation of what the user knows when performing well-learned tasks and has a number of confirmed behavioral correlates. Their analyses postulated that the number of productions (the number of rules needed to decompose goals into subgoals, to find methods to fit the subgoals, and to execute the sequence of actions in a method) necessary to perform a task is a good predictor of the time it takes to learn a system, that the number of productions that two systems have in common predicted the ease of learning the second after the first, that the number of productions used in constructing the next overt action predicted the delay from one overt action to the next, and that the number of items held temporarily in a working memory predicted the likelihood of errors or delays (Kieras and Bovair, 1985; Kieras and Polson, 1985; Polson and Kieras, 1984, 1985; Polson et al., 1986). Some of the predictions afforded by this specific analysis have been successfully tested; others are being tested now.

Though this approach is to be lauded for its specificity and the accuracy of some of its predictions, its weakness lies in determining how one counts the number of productions required for a task. Since production rule formalisms are general programming languages, a single function can be programmed in many ways. Consequently, for purposes of replicability, it is important for Kieras and Polson (1985) to specify further what production language style underlies these production analyses, and further, whether this style can be argued to be consonant with a the-oretically reasonable model of the architecture in which human information processing operates.

The chief limitation of the GOMS analysis is that it considers only error-free performance. This is a serious limitation since even skilled users spend at least a quarter of their time making and recovering from errors. In GOMS, goals are very specific to task situations; they are not currently in a general form (Card et al., 1983). This is not a limitation in principle, however, since GOMS is a deliberate simplification of Newell and Simon's (1972) general problem solver, a model that is general enough to describe any goal-directed behavior. Robertson (1983) suggests how error and error recovery could be incorporated into a GOMS-like analysis.

Rumelhart and Norman (1982) present a performance analysis of skilled typing that takes the description of errors as a primary concern. The treatment of errors in their analysis raises an important issue. In order to describe the occurrence of some kinds of errors, they were forced to change the assumption of how information is stored in memory. The analysis was fundamentally altered in order to qualitatively predict the typical errors for the task. This raises the question of whether GOMS, in which only error-free behavior was analyzed, embodies a representation that can be generalized to real performance that includes errors.

APPLYING WHAT WE KNOW OF THE USER'S KNOWLEDGE TO PRACTICAL PROBLEMS

The foregoing discussions have reviewed various representations of the user's knowledge of a system. We have described them in terms of the theoretical representations posited and some of the cognitive processes included in each type of analysis. It seems safe to conclude that while the area of research on users' mental representations is very active, it is not yet well developed (see the Research Recommendations section below). Nevertheless, software human factors is an applied area, and there is continual pressure to apply what we do know in this work to the task of design and training.

Applying what we know about mental representations to practical ends raises many questions. For example, if we knew what the user knew, how would we use this knowledge in design? Do we build the user interface to reflect a consistent mental model? If so, what does the input and presentation look like? Should we tell the learner what model to build?

DESIGNING INTERFACES

If the interface suggests or reflects an appropriate model, then the user could conceivably learn it with less guidance and perform it with fewer errors. The question is: What should the model be?

One approach to picking a model is to design user interfaces to accord with naive user conceptual models (Carroll and Thomas, 1982; Mayer and Bayman, 1981). Although this approach is simple and straightforward, its general utility is open to question. For example, Wright and Bason (1982) designed two software packages for a casual user population. One package was designed to be maximally consistent with the users' prior knowledge; users were asked how they thought about their data and what they wanted to be able to do with it, and this formed the basis for the user interface. The second package was also designed with input from potential users, but in this case, the designer used this information to determine how the users ought to think about their data and operations on it. The finding was that, in every way, the second package was a better design.

In a similar vein, Landauer et al. (1983) replaced the verbs in a word processor's command names (like append, substitute, and delete) with those that secretaries generated most often when describing to another secretary how to change a marked up manuscript (such as add, change, and omit). Paired associate learning theory would have predicted that these well-learned goal-action pairs from the secretaries' own vocabulary would have been good command names for secretaries learning a new word processor. The goal-action pairs are presumably preexisting paired associates, ones not needing new learning. Learning the word processor with these command names, however, was no better than learning the one with the system developers' names or even one with random names like allege, cypher, and deliberate. Naive users do not necessarily design better systems.

A variant of the naive model approach is to enter into the design process with a preconceived model, and then to iteratively build a prototype, test it, and refine the design (including the user's model) until acceptable usability is attained. This technique is the classic empirical approach (Dreyfus, 1955); it has been employed in recent designs that use the desktop metaphor in the interface for office systems (Bewley et al., 1983; Morgan et al., 1983), as well as in other application system designs (Gould and Boies, 1983; Wixon et al., 1983). The theoretical problem with this approach is that in the context of iterative and often radical redesign of a user interface, it is difficult to clearly separate the effect of the model on usability from that of other aspects of the redesign.[4]

A second design approach is to reduce the problem of communicating an appropriate conceptual model to the user by simplifying the system and its interface. DuBoulay et al. (1981) stress this in their characterization of a glass box model that consists of only a small number of components and interactions, all obviously reflected in the feedback that learners get from running the system. Carroll and Carrithers (1984) implemented this approach by providing new users with only a small but sufficient subset of commands to learn. This small set fits a relatively simple conceptual model. Carroll and Carrithers (1984) called this the "training wheels" approach, borrowing the analogy from learning to ride a bicycle. Once the subset of commands was learned, the user was gradually introduced to more complicated or more rarely used commands. This approach led to faster and more successful learning. An important question raised in this work, however, is how to decide which subset of commands is sufficient to do the task and fits a simple model. Furthermore, it raises the question of how to embellish the initially simplified conceptual model so that the change does not disrupt the learning the user has already accomplished.

A third design approach focuses on the method that the user learns rather than on the mental model. Moran (1981), Reisner (1981, 1984), and Young (1981) all stress the potential utility of task-oriented knowledge for design. Such knowledge can be represented formally. The suggestion is that these representations can be examined or manipulated prior to actual construction of the user interface to determine the least complex organization for

---

[4]However, Olson et al. (1984) highlight the importance of running prototype tests with two prototypes that differ in only one variable at a time, so that the effects of individual design changes can be measured independently.

the interface. For example, the designer can calculate values of merit for a system based on the number of rules in a grammar, the number of different terminal symbols, or various other metrics known in computational linguistics.This approach could also make it possible to define precisely concepts like consistency: similar tasks or goals should be associated with similar or identical actions (Moran, 1983). For example, deleting a sentence ought to have similar actions to deleting a paragraph. Empirical work has shown the importance of such concepts (e.g., Barnard et al., 1981; Black and Sebrechts, 1981; Thomas and Carroll, 1981; but see Landauer et al., 1984, for a caveat).

It should be noted that analysis of these relations, like consistency, may not go very far toward describing the interface design fully. For example, two interfaces with exactly the same grammatical description of a command language may have very different visual layouts. The visual layouts may lead to performance differences not predicted by a calculated complexity measure that is based only on inconsistencies in the command language. With the exception of Dunsmore (1986), most grammars do not represent features of visual layout that are known to be important. Dunsmore (1986) predicted and then experimentally verified that a crowded display would be more difficult for users to deal with than an uncrowded one. Furthermore, with the exception of Shneiderman (1982), whose multiparty grammars can be used to describe both a user's action and the system's response, there has been little attempt to integrate models of the various components of a system. Moreover, optimizing a design with respect to a task-oriented analysis will not necessarily include any of the design considerations that would be indicated by optimizing the presentation of a good mental model.

USER TRAINING

If a system has been built to conform to a consistent model or a well-formed set of methods, training may simply involve presenting the user with the model or methods. Several researchers have been concerned with developing techniques for providing users with appropriate conceptual models, something that even state-of-the-art instructional materials for software often fail to do (Bayman and Mayer, 1984; DuBoulay et al., 1981; Halasz and Moran, 1982). The benefits from presenting a mental model, however, are unclear.

Schlager and Ogden (1986), for example, incorporated both a method representation and a mental model in the training materials for teaching students how to form successful queries in a data base. For those specific query types that fit the model or methods presented, both representations speeded learning, regardless of whether the representation was a method representation or a mental model. Errors and difficulty occurred only when queries were different from the method or model taught.

Mayer (1976, 1981) provided students with a diagrammatic tool which incorporated a variety of concrete metaphors (e.g., input as a ticket window and storage as a file cabinet). Students who were exposed to this tool before studying a training manual were later able to perform better on both programming and recall tasks.

Kieras and Bovair (1984) taught people how a simple device worked either by a rote sequence of steps, with a model of the system, or with an analogy. The sequence of steps showed them what to do when. One model displayed what part was connected to another part beneath the surface, as if a flow diagram were painted on the control panel. The analogy described the control panel as being part of a mock spaceship, explaining what each control knob did in terms of battle-related actions. The results showed no benefit from either of the models over the rote sequence. On closer inspection, Kieras and Polson (1985) noted that neither of-the models gave the user any action-oriented help; the models merely gave a story about what the connections were, not how they worked.

Halasz and Moran (1982) taught students how to use a calculator using either a step-by-step action sequence to do standard calculations or instructions which included a verbal model of how the internal registers, windows, and stacks worked. They found that performance on standard tasks was identical for the two groups, but that the group who learned the model performed better on novel tasks.

Foss et al. (1982) provided a file folder metaphor to students learning to use a text editor. They found that students who were provided with the metaphor learned more in less time. In the same domain, Rumelhart and Norman (1981) used a composite of three metaphors: a secretary metaphor, which was used to explain that commands can be interspersed with text input; a card file metaphor, which was used to describe the deletion of a single numbered line from a file; and a tape recorder metaphor, which was used to convey the need for explicit terminators in files. Although performance was good overall, the fact that there were several metaphors produced cases in which a subject would employ one of the metaphors when another was appropriate.

Most of this work has focused on the use of mental models narrowly in training, namely, by telling the student the model or by providing simple and explicit advanced organizers (Ausubel, 1960). In another approach, an explicit mental model was prescribed; a system's training manual had a diagrammatic model of control flow for a menu-based system (Galambos et al., 1985). The resultant benefits were equivocal, however. Even greater integration between model and training appears necessary. The feasibility of this approach is exemplified in systems that have mental model analyses in their expert systems to interactively diagnose learner problems and to provide tailored support (e.g., Burton, 1981). No systematic behavioral studies have been carried out, however, to evaluate the effectiveness of this approach.

A more theoretical issue in the area of training pertains fundamentally to the nature of learning and the implications for designing training programs. One view of human learning and memory conceives of learning as an active process of problem solving in which concepts are created by the learner (e.g., Jenkins, 1974; Wittrock, 1974). This view contrasts with one in which learning is merely the storage of concepts in memory. In the latter view, a learner can be given a conceptual model explicitly (by diagram or a verbal explanation). In the active learning view, however, a conceptual model must be invented by the learner after an appropriate series of experiences.

Mayer (1980) adopted the active learner view. He asked learners to generate a metaphorical elaboration of programming statement types as they were learned. For example, after learning a FOR statement, the student was asked to describe its function using a metaphorical desktop vocabulary. He found that learners who had provided these elaborations were later able to perform better on novel and complex programming problems.

Carroll and Mack (1985) suggested that taking a serious active learning view raises the possibility that metaphors are useful not only when they provide familiar descriptions of novel experiences, but also when they provoke thought by failing to accord perfectly with the target of the metaphor comparison. Carroll and Mack

(1985) described a learner who was trying to learn a desktop interface and who initially tried to get a piece of paper from a paper pad icon by sweeping the cursor across the icon in a tearing motion. Here the desktop metaphor failed but also served to highlight effectively a specific fact about icon manipulation for the learner.

The active learning view provides a means of reconciling the observation that mental models are often chaotic and misconceived and the fact that users do often succeed in learning and using software. The suggestion is that people develop models that are good enough to suit their current goals. Defective conceptual models may ultimately play useful roles in learning and adequately support some user activity. It is an open question, however, whether they can actually facilitate learning and be used more effectively than more explicitly provided and more correct models (Mack et al., 1983).

RESEARCH RECOMMENDATIONS

These observations on the state of research and application of the concept of what the user knows lead to the following research recommendations.

1. *Detail what a mental model would consist of and how a person would use it to predict a system's behavior.* The term mental model has been used confusingly in the literature as referring to goal-oriented procedural knowledge, as well as knowledge about the components of the device, their functions, their relations to other components, and their workings. To date there have been no concrete characterizations of what a mental model is and how a person would run it to try out various simulated inputs. One attempt at this specification of a working mental model, a device model that is used for guiding external actions, resides in Davis's (1982) expert system for diagnosing electrical circuit failures. This model is used by the system to determine where physically a fault might be and, if it were at a particular location, what the device's expected behavior would be. Perhaps Davis's (1982) formalization of an internalized device model might serve as a base from which to build specifications of what a mental model would be and what mental operations would be necessary in order to use the mental model to make predictions about a system's behavior.

Yet, specifications of how a person would use a mental model to predict what a system will do is not sufficient to predict the user's behavior. Our understanding of mental models (if they exist) needs to be embedded in a model of a full-blown cognitive system, one that has problem-solving and decision-making processes that are sufficient to initiate the model runs, collect the results, and decide on an external action.

2. *Investigate whether people have and use mental models of various kinds.* Probably the most basic question in this area, still far from being answered, is whether people construct and use mental models at all. And, because of confusion of terminology in the literature, behavioral evidence is not clearly supportive. Even when we confine ourselves to the specific definition of mental models used in this report, however, there is little evidence that people have and use mental models. So far, the majority of evidence for mental models has come from people's self-reports that they form and use them (which may be post-hoc rationalizations), and from some evidence that when taught a system model or analogy, performance is sometimes better and learning may be faster. Specific research is needed to demonstrate whether people have models and that their behavior is clearly distinguishable from that produced by having stored sequence/method representations.

3. *Determine the behaviors that would demonstrate the model's form and the operations used on it.* If a person has a mental model, there may be some observable behavior that would give an analyst evidence of its form. Traditionally, experimental psychologists have made inferences about the existence of mental events by carefully constructing test situations with systematically varied features and observing particular overt responses such as the time that it takes to make a certain judgment or carry out an action, or the amount and kinds of errors made. The construction of the appropriate comparative test situations and the inferences that can be drawn from the responses, times, and errors must be based on a clearer notion of the form that the model might have and the processes that may act on it.

If the analyst can predict behavior knowing that the person has a mental model of a particular sort, then the analyst should be able to discover the mental models of other people from systematic examination of their behavior. Multidimensional scaling (Shepard et al., 1972), unfolding theory (Coombs, 1964), and ordered tree analysis (Reitman and Rueter, 1980) are examples of techniques that allow the analyst to infer particular mental representations from behavior. Perhaps aspects of behavior can reveal the form of a working mental model. This work could follow from a program of research that built on the theoretical work outlined above.

4. *Explore alternative views of sequence/method representations and the behavior predicted from them.* We currently have a better conception of what it means to have sequence/method representations and what processes may act on them to produce behavior than we do of mental models. GOMS represents the structure of goals, methods, and actions in a mental hierarchy for well-learned cognitive tasks. Kieras and Polson's (1985) production system formalism and its inference engine (a standard set of procedures for keeping track of where one is in a process and choosing the subsequent actions) is a concrete specification of this kind of knowledge and the processes that act on it. From that formalism follow concrete predictions of behavior, such as particular responses (key presses), their times, and the errors. A body of empirical data is growing, answering questions about which aspects of the representation affect behavior.

What is needed is more research in this vein. Formalisms of knowledge and operational mechanisms would be specified and the behavior of other kinds of sequence/method representations would be predicted. Empirical studies could then be formed to answer specific questions about the adequacy of the formalism, in detail, replacing the vague generalizations and contradictions that seem to plague research in this area today.

5. *Explore the types of mental representations that may exist that are not mechanistic.* Most of the mental models that are conceived in this research are mechanistic in nature. The sequence/method representations are mechanistic and serial. These consist of components and processes that mimic physical devices. There may be mental representations of other types, however, that drive people's exploratory and explanatory behavior. People claim to make inferences and explorations from stored visual and auditory images; mathematicians experiment mentally with computational systems, making inferences before showing any external behavior; people likely reason at different levels of abstraction about a system, making inferences of a very general nature in planning before exploring details in a step-by-step fashion. There

may be visual, auditory, computational, or hierarchical systems that form helpful bases for people's reasoning. These other possible types of mental representations should be made concrete, and their behavioral correlates should be explored.

6. *Determine how people intermix different representations in producing behavior.* This report has reviewed a variety of types of knowledge that may be held by a user of a computer system. It is likely that users have some knowledge stored in several of these representations: some well-known procedures for executing simple sequences; some well-formed GOMS-like structures for doing familiar but more complicated tasks; and some mental models that help the user explore alternative actions to take when an error occurs or when a novel task is presented to them. If all of these representations exist simultaneously, then we need to know when each is used and how the person moves between them and/or combines their operations or products. There is likely to be some problem-solving or decision-making apparatus that guides the overall task behavior, sometimes exploring unknown territory with a process like means-ends analysis or running a mental model, and other times executing well-learned actions from stored goal structures (see, for example, the extensive literature on automaticity; Shiffrin and Schneider, 1977). An integrated performance view is called for.

7. *Explore how knowledge about systems is acquired.* If we can discover the form of the representation of knowledge that people have about computer systems, we would like also to know how that information was acquired. Lewis's work (1986) on how people make inferences about a system from watching its behavior is a good example of how to specify concretely how people learn complicated tasks on computers. Work is also needed on how people acquire mental models, simple sequences, and methods. This work would have an impact not only on the design of systems and their training, but also would give some basic knowledge about the problem of learning complex behavior in general.

8. *Determine how individual differences have an impact on learning of and performance on systems.* Individuals' cognitive capacities differ, making different computer users more and less capable. Some of these differences are likely to arise from simply having more knowledge from longer exposure to the system. Exposure could provide a user with more task knowledge as well as more

specific and more accurate mental models. Some of the differences in performance, however, may arise from basic individual differences in abilities. For example, Gomez et al. (1983) have shown that people who are not good at visual memory have difficulty with some word processors. Further, they found that a system that required less recall of a command syntax reduced the performance differences found between those who could recall locations and those who could not. We need to know more about individual cognitive differences and their concomitant effect on people's mental representations of and performance on complex tasks. The results will have implications for both the design of systems and the construction of training sequences for a particular system for particular users.

9. *Explore the design of training sequences for systems.* A related training issue surrounds the idea of "training wheels," the notion that a scaled-down system is easier to learn initially. Specifying and analyzing the mental model or sequence/method representations implied by the scaled-down system may lead designers to build more coherent systems and more effective training sequences. Further, this analysis may indicate how information about the full system should be taught as an add-on to the training wheels system.

10. *Provide system designers with tools to help them develop interfaces that invoke good representations in users.* There is probably some guidance that can be provided to systems designers while they design the user interface to ensure that the sequence/method representation or the mental model will be an effective guide to accurate performance. Such tools may come in the form of user interface management systems; which constrain the design set. The goal may be to constrain the ways that the designers can display things or constrain the ways that they can allow the user to invoke a command so that a coherent, easily understood set is formed, one that invokes in the user a good mental model or a coherent set of goal-actions pairs. Designing these guidance tools is an important research topic, one that can aid the transfer of technology from the laboratory to the design and development arena.

11. *Expand the task domain to more complex software.* Most of the research in the area of mental models and sequence/method representations for human-computer interaction has focused on text processing and simple device models. Whatever results

emerge from these areas should be tested for their applicability to more complex, nonexclusively text-based tasks, such as graphics design, tactical decision making, project planning and tracking, and data base query. It is likely that the complexity of these tasks, in which the user is almost never doing a task that is well-learned, requires the user to use mental models and to try out actions never used before. These may be ideal domains in which to test notions of the use of mental models, the productive interaction of sequence/method representations and mental models, and the involvement of general problem-solving skills, reasoning, and decision making.

REFERENCES

Adelson, B. (1981) Problem solving and the development of abstract categories in programming languages. *Memory and Cognition,* 9, 422-433.

Ausubel, D. P. (1960) The use of advance organizers in the learning and retention of meaningful verbal material. *Journal of Educational Psychology,* 51, 267-272.

Barnard, P. J., Hammond, N. V., Morton, J., Long, J. B., and Clark, I. A. (1981) Consistency and compatibility in human-computer dialogue. *International Journal of Man-Machine Studies,* 15, 87-134.

Baron, S., and Levison, W. H. (1980) The optimal control model: Status and future direction. *Proceedings of IEEE Conference on Cybernetics and Society.* Cambridge, MA.

Bayman, P., and Mayer, R. E. (1984) Instructional manipulation of users' mental models for electronic calculators. *International Journal of Man-Machine Studies,* 20, 189-199.

Bewley, W. L., Roberts, T. L., Schroit, D., and Verplank, W. L. (1983) Human factors testing of Xerox's 8010 "Star" Office Workstation. *Proceedings of the 1983 CHI Conference on Human Factors in Computing.* New York: Association of Computing Machinery.

Black, J. B., and Sebrechts, M. M. (1981) Facilitating human-computer communication. *Applied Psycholinguistics,* 2, 87-134.

Bott, R. (1979) A study in complex learning: Theory and methodology. Report 82. Center for Human Information Processing, University of California at San Diego, La Jolla, CA.

Burton, R. B. (1981) DEBUGGY: Diagnosing bugs in a simple procedural skill. In D. H. Sleeman and J. S. Brown (eds.), *Intelligent Tutoring Systems.* London: Academic Press.

Card, S. K., Moran, T. P., and Newell, A. (1980a) Computer text editing: An information processing analysis of a routine cognitive skill. *Cognitive Psychology,* 12, 32-74.

Card, S. K., Moran, T. P., and Newell, A. (1980b) The keystroke level model for user performance time with interactive systems. *Communications of the ACM,* 23, 396-410.

REFERENCES

Card, S. K., Moran, T. P., and Newell, A. (1983) *The Psychology of Human-Computer Interaction.* Hillsdale, NJ: Erlbaum.

Carroll, J. M., and Carrithers, C. (1984) Training wheels in a user interface. *Communications of the ACM,* 27, 800-806.

Carroll, J. M., and Mack, R. L. (1985) Metaphor, computing systems, and active learning. *International Journal of Man-Machine Studies,* 22, 39-57.

Carroll, J. M., and Thomas, J. C. (1982) Metaphor and the cognitive representation of computing systems. *IEEE Transactions on Systems, Man, and Cybernetics,* SMC-12, 107-116.

Chase, W. G., and Simon, H. A. (1973) Perception in chess. *Cognitive Psychology,* 4, 55-81.

Coombs, C. H. (1964) *A Theory of Data.* New York: John Wiley & Sons.

Davis, R. (1982) Expert systems: Where are we? And, where do we go from here? *The AI Magazine,* Spring, 3-22.

Douglas, S. A., and Moran, T. P. (1983) Learning text editor semantics by analogy. *Proceedings of the 1983 CHI Conference on Human Factors in Computing.* New York: Association of Computing Machinery.

Dreyfus, H. (1955) *Designing for People.* New York: Simon & Schuster.

DuBoulay, B., O'Shea, T., and Monk, J. (1981) The black box inside the glass box: Presenting computing concepts to novices. *International Journal of Man-Machine Studies,* 14, 237-249.

Dunsmore, H. E. (1986) A formal grammar approach to human factors research. Technical Report 623, Department of Computer Science, Purdue University, West Lafayette, IN.

Egan, D. E., and Schwartz, B. J. (1979) Chunking in recall of symbolic drawings. *Memory and Cognition,* 7, 149-158.

Ehrlich, K., and Soloway, E. (1984) An empirical investigation of the tacit plan knowledge in programming. In J. Thomas and M. Schneider (eds.), *Human Factors in Computing Systems.* Norwood, NJ: Ablex.

Embley, D. W., Lan, N. T., Leinbaugh, D. W., and Nagy, G. (1978) A procedure for predicting program editor performance from the users point of view. *International Journal of Man-Machine Studies,* 10, 639-650.

Fodor, J. A., Bever, T. G., and Garrett, M. F. (1974) *The Psychology of Language.* New York: McGraw-Hill.

Foley, L. J., and Williges, R. C. (1982) User models of text editing command languages. *Human Factors in Computer Systems Proceedings.* Washington, DC: National Bureau of Standards.

Foss, D. J., Rosson, M. B., and Smith, P. L. (1982) Reducing manual labor: An experimental analysis of learning aids for a texteditor. *Human Factors in Computer Systems Proceedings.* Washington, DC: National Bureau of Standards.

Galambos, J. A., Sebrechts, M. M., Wikler, E. S., and Black, J. B. (1985) A diagrammatic language for instruction of a menu-based word processing system. In S. Williams (ed.), *Humans and Machines: The Interface Through Language.* Norwood, NJ: Ablex.

Gomez, L. M., Egan, D. E., Wheeler, E. A., Sharma, D. K., and Gruchacz, A.M. (1983) How interface design determines who has difficulty learning to use a text editor. Pp. 176-179 in *Proceedings of the 1983 CHI Conference on Human Factors in Computing.* New York: Association of Computing Machinery.

REFERENCES

Gould, J. D., and Boies, S. J. (1983) Human factors challenges in creating a principal support office system-the speech filing approach. *ACM Transactions on Office Information Systems,* 1, 273-298.

Halasz, F., and Moran, T. P. (1982) Analogy considered harmful. *Human Factors in Computer Systems Proceedings.* Washington, DC: National Bureau of Standards.

Hilgard, E. R., and Bower, G. H. (1975) *Theories of Learning.* Englewood Cliffs, NJ: Prentice-Hall.

Jagacinski, R. J., and Miller, R. A. (1978) Describing the human operator's internal model of a dynamic system. *Human Factors,* 20, 425-433.

Jagacinski, R. J., Plamondon, B. D., and Miller, R. A. (in press) Describing movement at two levels of abstraction. In P. A. Hancock (ed.), *Human Factors Psychology.* Amsterdam: North-Holland.

Jenkins, J. J. (1974) Remember that old theory of memory? Well, forget it! *American Psychologist,* 29, 785-795.

Kieras, D. E., and Bovair, S. (1984) The role of a mental model in learning to operate a device. *Cognitive Science,* 8, 255-274.

Kieras, D. E., and Bovair, S. (1986) A production system analysis of transfer of training. *Journal of Memory and Language,* 25, 507-524.

Kieras, D. E., and Polson, P. G. (1983) A generalized transition network representation for interactive systems. Pp. 103-106. *Proceedings of the 1983 CHI Conference on Human Factors in Computing.* New York: Association of Computing Machinery.

Kieras, D. E., and Polson, P. G. (1985) An approach to the formal analysis of user complexity. *International Journal of Man-Machine Studies,* 22, 365-394.

Kraut, R. E., Hanson, S. J., and Farber, J. M. (1983) Command use and interface design. *Proceedings of the 1983 CHI Conference on Human Factors in Computing.* New York: Association of Computing Machinery.

Landauer, T. K., Galotti, K. M., and Hartwell, S. (1983) Natural command names and initial learning: A study of text-editing terms. *Communications of the Association of Computing Machinery,* 26, 495-503.

Landauer, T. K., Galotti, K. M., and Hartwell, S. (1984) What makes a difference when? Comments on Grudin and Bernard. *Human Factors,* 26(4), 423-429.

Lewis, C. (1986) A model of mental model construction. *Proceedings of the 1986 CHI Conference on Human Factors in Computing.* New York: Association of Computing Machinery.

Mack, R. L., Lewis, C. H., and Carroll, J. M. (1983) Learning to use word processors: Problems and prospects. *ACM Transactions on Office Information Systems,* 1, 254-271.

Mantei, M. (1982) *Disorientation Behavior in Person-Computer Interaction.* Unpublished PhD dissertation. Department of Communication, University of Southern California.

Mayer, R. E. (1976) Some conditions of meaningful learning for computer programming: Advance organizers and subject control of frame order. *Journal of Educational Psychology,* 67, 725-734.

Mayer, R. E. (1980) Elaboration techniques for technical text: An experimental test of the learning strategy hypothesis. *Journal of Educational Psychology,* 72, 770-784.

Mayer, R. E. (1981) The psychology of how novices learn computer programming. *Computing Surveys,* 13, 121-141.

REFERENCES

Mayer, R. E., and Bayman, P. (1981) Psychology of calculator languages: A framework for describing differences in users' knowledge. *Communications of the ACM,* 24, 511-520.

McKeithen, K. B., Reitman, J. S., Rueter, H. H., and Hirtle, S. C. (1981) Knowledge organization and skill differences in computer programming. *Cognitive Psychology,* 13, 307-325.

Miller, G. A. (1962) Some psychological studies of grammar. *American Psychologist,* 17, 748-762.

Miller, R. A. (1985) A systems approach to modeling discrete control performance. In W. B. Rouse (ed.), *Advances in Man-Machine Systems Research,* Volume 2. Greenwich, CT: JAI Press.

Moran, T. P. (1981) The command language grammar: A representation for the user interface of interaction computer systems. *International Journal of Man-Machine Studies,* 15, 3-50.

Moran, T. P. (1983) Getting into a system: External-internal task mapping analysis. Pp. 45-49 in *Proceedings of the 1983 CHI Conference on Human Factors in Computing.* New York: Association of Computing Machinery.

Morgan, C., Williams, G., and Lemmons, P. (1983) An interview with Wayne Rosing, Bruce Daniels, and Larry Tesler. *BYTE,* February, 33-50.

Newell, A., and Simon, H. A. (1972) *Human Problem Solving.* Englewood Cliffs, NJ: Prentice-Hall.

Norman, D. A. (1983) Some observations on mental models. In D. Gentner and A. Stevens (eds.), *Mental Models.* Hillsdale, NJ: Erlbaum.

Olson, J. Reitman (1987) Cognitive analysis of people's use of software. In J. Carroll (ed.), *Interfacing Thought: Cognitive Aspects of Human-Computer Interaction.* Cambridge, MA: Bradley Books/MIT Press.

Olson, J. Reitman, and E. Nilsen (1988) Cognitive analysis of people's use of spreadsheet software Technical Report. *Human-Computer Interaction,* 1988, in press.

Olson, J. Reitman, Whitten, W. B., II, and Gruenenfelder, T. M. (1984) A general user interface for creating and displaying tree-structures, hierarchies, decision trees, and nested menus. In Y. Vassiliou (ed.), *Human Factors and Interactive Computer Systems.* Norwood, NJ: Ablex.

Payne, S. J., and Green, T. R. G. (1983) The user's perception of the interaction language: A two-level model. *Proceedings of the 1983 CHI Conference on Human Factors in Computing.* New York: Association of Computing Machinery.

Pew, R. W., and Baron, S. (1983) Perspectives on human performance modeling. *Automatica,* 19, 663-676.

Polson, P. G., and Kieras, D. E. (1984). A formal description of user's knowledge of how to operate at device and user complexity. *Behavior Research Methods, Instruments, and Computers,* 16, 249-255.

Polson, P. G., and Kieras, D. E. (1985) A quantitative model of the learning and performance of text editing knowledge. *Proceedings of the 1985 CHI Conference on Human Factors in Computing.* New York: Association of Computing Machinery.

Polson, P. G., Muncher, E., and Engelbeck, G. (1986) A test of a common elements theory of transfer. *Proceedings of the 1986 CHI Conference on Human Factors in Computing.* New York: Association of Computing Machinery.

REFERENCES

Postman, L., and Stark, K. (1969) Role of response availability in transfer and interference. *Journal of Experimental Psychology*, 79, 168-177.

Rasmussen, J. (1983) Skills, rules, and knowledge: Signals, signs, and symbols, and other distinctions in human performance models. *IEEE Transactions on Systems, Man, and Cybernetics*, SMC-13, 257-266.

Reisner, P. (1981) Formal grammar and human factors design of an interactive graphics system. *IEEE Transactions of Software Engineering*, SE-7, 229-240.

Reisner, P. (1983) Analytic tools for human factors software. In A. Blaser and M. Zoeppritz (eds.), *End-User Systems and Their Human Factors*. Proceedings of the scientific symposium conducted on the occasion of the 15th anniversary of the Science Center Heidelberg of IBM Germany, in G. Goos and J. Hartmanis (eds.), *Lecture Notes in Computer Science*, Series No. 150. Berlin: Springer-Verlag.

Reisner, P. (1984) Formal grammar as a tool for analyzing ease of use: Some fundamental concepts. P. 53 in J. Thomas and M. Schneider (eds.), *Human Factors in Computing Systems*. Norwood, NJ: Ablex.

Reitman, J. S. (1976) Skilled perception in Go: Deducing memory structures from inter-response times. *Cognitive Psychology*, 8, 336-377.

Reitman, J. S., and Rueter, H. H. (1980) Organization revealed by recall orders and confirmed by pauses. *Cognitive Psychology*, 12, 554-581.

Robertson, S. R. (1983) *Goal, Plan, and Outcome Tracking in Computer Text-Editing Performance*. Cognitive Science Technical Report 25. Yale University, New Haven, CT.

Rosson, M. B. (1983) Patterns of experience in text editing. Pp. 171-175 in *Proceedings of the 1983 CHI Conference on Human Factors in Computing*. New York: Association of Computing Machinery.

Rouse, W. B., and Morris, N. M. (1986) On looking into the black box: Prospects and limits in the search for mental models. *Psychological Bulletin*, Vol. 100, No. 3, pp. 349-363.

Rumelhart, D. E., and Norman, D. A. (1981) Analogical processes in learning. In J. R. Anderson (ed.), *Cognitive Skills and Their Acquisition*. Hillsdale, NJ: Erlbaum.

Rumelhart, D. E., and Norman, D. A. (1982) Simulating a skilled typist: A study of skilled cognitive-motor performance. *Cognitive Science*, 6, 1-36.

Scandura, A. M., Lowerre, G. F., Veneski, J., and Scandura, J. M. (1976) Using electronic calculators with elementary children. *Educational Technology*, 16, 14-18.

Schlager, M. S., and Ogden, W. C. (1986) A cognitive model of database querying: A tool for novice instruction. *Proceedings of the 1986 CHI Conference on Human Factors in Computing*. New York: Association of Computing Machinery.

Shepard, R. N., Romney, A. K., and Nerlove, S. B. (1972) *Multidimensional Scaling: Theory and Applications in the Behavioral Sciences*. New York: Seminar Press.

Sheridan, T. B., Charny, L., Mendel, M. B., and Roseborough, J. B. (1986) Supervisory Control, Mental Models, and Decision Aids. MIT Department of Mechanical Engineering Technical Report, July. Massachusetts Institute of Technology.

Shiffrin, R. M., and Schneider, W. (1977) Controlled and automatic human information processing. *Psychological Review*, 84, 127-190.

REFERENCES

Shneiderman, B. (1980) Software Psychology: *Human Factors of Computer and Information Systems.* Cambridge: Winthrop.

Shneiderman, G. (1982) Multiparty grammars and related features for defining interactive systems. *IEEE Transactions on Systems, Man, and Cybernetics,* SMC-12, 2.

Shrager, J., and Klahr, D. (1983) Learning in an instructionless environment: Observation and analysis. *Proceedings of the 1983 CHI Conference on Human Factors in Computing.* New York: Association of Computing Machinery.

Smelcer, J. B. (1986) Expertise in data modeling or what is inside the head of an expert data modeler? *Proceedings of the 1986 CHI Conference on Human Factors in Computing.* New York: Association of Computing Machinery.

Thomas, J. C., and Carroll, J. M. (1981) Human factors in communication. *IBM Systems Journal,* 20, 237-263.

Veldhuyzen, W., and Stassen, H. G. (1976) The internal models: What does it mean in human control. In T. B. Sheridan and G. Johannsen (eds.), *Monitoring Behavior and Supervisory Control.* New York: Plenum.

Whiteside, J., and Wixon, D. (1984) Developmental theory as a framework for studying human-computer interaction. In H. R. Hartson (ed.), *Advances in Human-Computer Interaction.* Norwood, NJ: Ablex.

Wittrock, M. C. (1974) Learning as a generative process. *Educational Psychology,* 11, 87-95.

Wright, P., and Bason, G. (1982) Detour routes to usability: A comparison of alternative approaches to multipurpose software design. *International Journal of Man-Machine Studies,* 18, 391-400.

Young, R. M. (1981) The machine inside the machine: Users' models of pocket calculators. *International Journal of Man-Machine Studies,* 15, 51-85.

Young, R. M. (1983) Surrogates and mappings: Two kinds of conceptual models for interactive devices. In D. Gentner and A. Stevens (eds.), *Mental Models.* Hillsdale, NJ: Erlbaum.